DISECONOMIES OF SCALE IN PUBLIC EDUCATION: A RATIONAL FOR SCHOOL VOUCHERS

Donald P. Lade, M.B.A., Ph.D.

DISECONOMIES OF SCALE IN PUBLIC EDUCATION: A RATIONAL FOR SCHOOL VOUCHERS

A Study –And Theory– Based on Operational Budget Secrets in the Public Schools, Including an Example of Bureaucratic Growth in the Post World War II Climate of Economic Expansion

Donald P. Lade, M.B.A., Ph.D.

Copyright © 2003 by Donald P. Lade.

Library of Congress Number: 2003093371
ISBN: 1-4134-1096-0

This book was printed in the United States of America.

To order additional copies of this book, contact:
Xlibris Corporation
1-888-795-4274
www.Xlibris.com
Orders@Xlibris.com
18397

CONTENTS

FIGURES

INTRODUCTION

The (pro) school voucher issue could use some help from an unexpected source—public school district budgets themselves. And, while the school-choice movement is getting smarter, there has yet to be a really serious assault on the public school monopoly using the voucher mechanism. This is not news. One part of this problem has been the lack of a means to link school district budgets, budget cost factors, and voter awareness together—especially in an historical, generational time frame for budgets and costs tied to a long-range commitment for voter interests.

One purpose of this study is to bring certain ideas and historical facts together with some conceptual tools to focus on public school district budgets and economics with a view to the voucher issue and the school-choice movement. One salient fact for this combination is that school district budgets live in a world of shadows, at the very least so far as the voting public is concerned. Another fact is that the cost basis for these budgets is even more obscure. Thus, it is hard for voters to see what school vouchers are going to pay for; and, even worse, what costs have been incorporated into the public education bill over generations past. Of course, another part of the situation is the fact that private school budgets were never meant for public voter scrutiny. But surprisingly, a major and key factor in the voucher issue is the extent of the increasing cost basis for the public schools since World War II alone.

Successive sections of this study are going to take a look at school district budgets, their economics and governance, the post World War II growth in the American public school system, and some of the personnel numbers that relate to school district staff and their growth. These last are going to be a (more) theoretical rational to show how and why there could be a budget and cost evolution for the public school system over the years, using one very important, large scale example in California. This rational is based on an ability to analyze the internal details of a school district budget over a period of many years, every year taken one at a time and together. This is the key to dealing with public school bureaucracies.

Another major point that must be brought up front to the voting public is the fact that *vouchers* are a choice mechanism or plan for a choice system that is advocated by the school choice movement. The foundation idea here is to create an educational system that lies primarily *beyond* what public authority in education is doing now (Chubb and Moe, 1990). And another aspect to vouchers must be recognized, but perhaps not emphasized. And that aspect of the issue is the fact that the technical details of voucher initiatives will determine the extent to which they will work to approach a free market system in education (Lieberman, 1993). However, this study has been prepared to use historical public school budgets to emphasize the cost basis for the public schools to show how and where costs and benefits can be matched to vouchers within a choice system. That is, how taxes (present costs) can be compared to hypothetical vouchers (future prices) in a new market system of school-choice. If "Conant was wrong," then vouchers can save a lot of time, money, school reform rhetoric, and half measures (Toch, 1991). And this reminds us that schools can tax, but vouchers can pass—maybe sooner, rather than later.

THE BUDGET CURTAIN
OF SHADOWS

The foundation aspect of this study is its use as a basic primer to the arcane, but conceptually simple, world of public school district budgeting. Annual budgeting is the public school mechanism and method for cost basis funding; and, the possibility that public education has been over funded is widely recognized but little understood (Lieberman, 1993). The fact that there could be hidden school district operational agendas, costs, objectives, and programs residing in the budgets that boards of education approve year in and year out should not come as a real surprise to thinking readers. It is common (sense) knowledge throughout the country that large portions of school district budgets are essentially discretionary, but few can demonstrate just how and why this is the case—and, almost without exception these few are current player insiders. Often foundation costs, mandated costs, and discretionary costs are subsumed under budget costs and program or structure requirements (Bidwell and Kasarda, 1985, 1987), and accepted as total base costs by the media and the public.

One exciting new way to get beyond this curtain and shadows of the school budget system is to have historical records that would allow one to track the development of school district expenditure budgets over a relatively long period during their evolution. These are the records that essentially die with the players in the public schools as the internal school district budget apparatus is passed from generation to generation of school district administrators. The curriculum management and supervision component of one such budget is analyzed in the diseconomies of scales section of this study. But, any and all parts of a school district budget could be worked in the same way.

Now, a public school district in the United States must be of a fair size for it to begin to extract a measure of budget control unto itself and away from the immediate control of the local board of education. If the members of the local board can count the teachers on their fingers and toes, they will tend to do the budget themselves, in spite of whatever the superintendent and the administrative staff may do. Even so, board members must actually go through each and every item in the budget in one way or another in order to know what is altogether in the budget. One original premise behind local, community school districts was local control; and, budget control was to be an essential element of local control. Further, this was supposed to be a form of cost control. Actually, it was more nearly cost control at the margin; and, even in the public schools, there are additional costs involved beyond the annual, funds budget (Lieberman, 1993). However, once the reader starts looking about in the local public school district budget world, various erosions of budget control are usually easy to find. But the real thrust of this study example lies in the middle to large sized districts where there exists a definite middle ground between teachers and board members. And, especially in these districts, the tendency in the post World War II years has been to build costs into the budget on a discretionary basis similar to cost-plus contracting using a monopoly market condition and the power to tax at cost-plus what has essentially amounted to a total benefits employee package. With the budget existing as an obscure account vehicle, these tendencies have been masked from the media and the public to a large extent. It is easy to study how this has come to pass using historical budget records.

This school budget and economics primer also highlights some ways in which the public common sense has been defied by esoteric budget mastications in many public school districts during the years of general growth in public education after World War II. And, strangely enough, it is the Catholic schools that can provide an additional point of navigation in these waters because they can operate at the same levels of scale (Chubb and Moe, 1990), although the plan of this primer will not be to detail a comparison between public and parochial schools (Lieberman, 1993). But surprisingly enough, over the last thirty years, the Catholic schools have been seen to be doing better with budget less, under conditions of declining enrollment. In other words, in direct contrast to the public expectations of the public schools *and* at the mass education scale. This is merely one of the juxtapositions that can be brought to the fore as an example to show that there are easy to discover disparities in the application of budget resources to large scale education in America. Ones that thinking Americans intuitively know about, but find difficult to penetrate behind the budget

curtain of shadows used by the majority of the established public school district bureaucracies.

Also surprisingly, it is the Catholic schools that can point the way to additional dimensions in the application of free (or freer) markets to public education because of their size and abilities to capture market share while, at the same time, they are not in the same league with the so-called elite private schools commanding especially high levels of resource inputs. Actually, the diseconomies of scale example presented later in this primer will demonstrate a heavy correlation between management structure and curriculum costs coincident with mildly negative results in educational product over an extended period of time in the public schools. Of course, budgeting schedules in the public schools are conducive to this type of self-generating inefficiency, and program costs tend (as above) to assume a life of their own (Lieberman, 1993). Yet, often enough, the budgets themselves will tend to obscure these inefficiencies and costs, even though these board of education approved budgets are, in fact, public documents when they are published and distributed. These budgets show a schedule of costs and taxes at which vouchers can pass. More importantly, vouchers could also pass for less.

BUDGET BASICS, FRESHMAN ECONOMICS, AND GOOD GOVERNMENT FOR THE PUBLIC SCHOOLS

Traditional public school district budgets present the basic line items and position details to cost (out) district programs, but, their legitimacy in the past has depended on a constituency belief in economies of scale and a political justification for monopoly control. Under this rational, the bigger and better the school systems grew to become, the more efficient they could emerge due to economies of scale (Cohn, 1972; Blaug, 1985). This rational and reason reached a popular crescendo with James B. Conant's "comprehensive high school" report in 1959; but, the economies of scale idea has always loomed large in the budget background for the public schools, even today. Comprehensive schools also emphasized comprehensive curriculum; and, the institutionalization of curriculum development and management had already been heavily worked by the public schools for at least a generation by the time of the report.[1] So, by the 1960's there was a budget foundation for large scale, comprehensive spectrum, curriculum justified cost-plus funding for the public schools.

In addition, the political justification for monopoly control had been concurrently factored into these developments as education by curriculum, comprehensive economies, and good governance in the administration of public school systems by using highly legitimized budget categories, components, and levels of funding, (which also meant spending and taxing). It became even more widely accepted that these school systems administered as local public school districts under state control would not exhibit monopoly pricing diseconomies deriving from monopoly control because local and state governance would insure efficiencies in their administration through diligent and effective oversight. Thus, the systems would be big, comprehensive, economical, educationally effective in curriculum, and efficient. So, as school districts grew and prospered, they could put more resources (mostly money) into the educational mill, but they would not charge monopoly prices because educationally inefficient expenses would be controlled by the oversight responsibilities of local and state government. Of course, in this scheme of things, there would be no need or place for market mechanisms in public education, let alone free markets or vouchers. And clients, constituents, and voters would be happy.

The preceding conception of cost and expense budgeting was easy to sell during the various growth and reform periods in American public education, beginning right with the Industrial Revolution. It was essentially freshman economics applied to good government. It made good sense and few voters questioned it, especially at the polls. So, the public school system of budget and cost spread across the country, gathering momentum and speed. The steam behind this locomotive was a long and steady history of increasing budgeting and funding levels for the schools based on antecedent revenue streams. More and more money was getting into public education, in one way or another, where it could be spent how and where local boards of education and their staffs wanted it to be spent; and, the vehicle for this spending was the annually approved and balanced public school district budget. The same budget that is now the veil of tears for many districts where disruptions in historical revenue streams have occurred. Yet, these are bottom line tears, because most of the budget details and line listings that remain in these budgets lie behind the curtain of shadows (above) of what are, even today, essentially historical growth budgets.

But still, the budget seems to come first in the public schools, not the revenue. And the schools have been able to distance and disassociate revenue from cost and tax. This is one reason that the school-choice movement has had difficulty pricing vouchers. The acceptance of (historical) budget-first pricing for the public schools has been part of the myth and mystique that has come to surround the public school budget and its so called annual budgeting process or cycle. This phenomenon extends to even the state level where it often adds sum-of-the-parts mandates and requirements. In other words, budget expenditures tend to be thought of as the reason for revenues to support these expenditures. So it is seen that "it is in the budget," and "it has been cut from the budget," or "it has been added to the budget" as opposed to seeing the budget as an accounting vehicle for educational programs. One of the things that this budget folklore means for voters is that budget details, listings, methods, and procedures in school districts have to be understood in order to see what might happen to income streams as they pass through the schools to become expenditure costs. To pass, vouchers (people) should more tightly focus on these past, present, and future costs.

OPERATIONAL BUDGET WHATS AND WHYS IN A CLIMATE OF ECONOMIC EXPANSION

Since this is a primer for past school budget costs and economics of production focusing on future tax revenues and voucher pricing, there will not be an attempt to look at all aspects of district level budgets or the entire budget process as it occurs each and every year. So, there will also be no attempt to try and describe everything that can happen to the money that resides in public school district budgets. But, there will be a description of some of the common things that do happen to these funds; and, there are going to be examples showing how and why these things can and do happen. To be able to do this, there must be available a set of historical school district budget records (above), because no single year (or even two or three years) of budget history can clearly show the many possible transformations of budgeted funds from one application to another that can occur in any given school district during and between fiscal years. For various reasons and in various ways, it has long been possible and practice to transfer such things as teacher funds into equipment orders, and equipment line items back into teachers again. This is just one example. However, it has been more usual (and easier) to transfer teachers into custodians and custodians into instructional aids, but such things lead deep inside the budget. In fact, capital outlay allocations and transportation expenditures are subjects in themselves. Yet, these are some of the operational whats and whys in the administration of a district budget that will not be emphasized here.

Many of the notions found in this study have their origin in the above historical budget records, mostly from public school districts in Southern California. Coincidentally, the Los Angeles Basin and its (now) metropolitan area has several natural advantages that accrue to the study of public school district budgets and economics. One is its history of population and economic expansion after World War II; and, another has been the relatively unsophisticated (pure) state of local political affairs that existed for the area between World War I and World War II, especially when compared to other major big city areas of public education interest in the United States such as Boston, Chicago, and New York. During the Progressive Era (Southern) California became a showpiece for the development of educational institutions and reform improvements thereto in the public interest and in tune with the true spirit of the "one best system" (Tyack, 1974; Chubb and Moe, 1990). Even so, the findings found in this study are not limited to such districts as those found in Southern California, as the inspection of district budgets from other areas of the country would quickly show (Toch, 1991). Yet, over the years, the California led one best system became acknowledged as a popularized model of the Progressive Era spirit in public education taken at its best (Tyack, 1974). Obviously, the budgets themselves show exactly what went on during the period; but, then and now, California remained near the acknowledged forefront of positive initiatives in public education (Lieberman, 1993). In fact, the Southern California social situation from the mid-1940's to the mid-1970's became case study dream for anyone who wanted to examine the whats and whys of public school district budget and expenditure development during an extended period of progressive spirit, good government, and economic expansion. And the continuous economic expansion and population growth gave almost everything a positive and monotonic increasing upward bias.

To examine this period of expansion with respect to what happened inside a given school district, there would have to be an analysis of the changes that took place in the various elements of the budget, year-by-year, for this district over a period of a generation or longer. So, a string of historical budget records (above) over a period of 20 to 30 years would be needed. One reason for this is the fact that most higher level budget administrators in the public schools reach their positions of budget cycle experience and knowledge only later in their careers, perform in budget administration duties for a lesser number of years, and then retire—never having the inclination or intent to do historical (longitudinal) budget studies (below). So, it should be no surprise that their district budget knowledge, which is gained almost entirely through practice in the position, tends to die with them, especially since there is no legal requirement to maintain (or read) historical budget files. On the contrary, in public school districts, budgeting is one year at a time and that is all there is to it.

Further, in contrast to many members of the board of directors of major American corporations, the members of the local boards of education in American public school districts most usually have very limited operational budget experience and their level (whatever) of experience and budget knowledge tends to be well below that of the district budget administration who provide the budgets that board members annually and incrementally approve. Actually, this state of affairs is widely acknowledged by all players, except the voting public is usually not fully aware of the magnitude of the situation and its impact on tax trends. So, for public school board members, historical records are moot and the budget basis origins for current and recent year budgets are usually obscure right down to line items and position details. In fact, a fiscal management system like zero-base budgeting would be akin to something from science fiction for the public schools at the local level.

Now, this obscurity factor for the budget has been one of the reasons why members of local boards have been treated as passing players by district budget administrators; and, it is one of the reasons why obfuscation practices on the part of district officials can creep into the picture and initiate tendencies that exacerbate this situation. Local school boards just are not constructed to create a Bureau of the Budget, or a Congressional Budget Office, or a General Accounting Office. Such are supposed to be part of the state level oversight function (above). In addition, budget administrators tend to have vested interests in the budget, and probably a few skeletons in the closet, while board members tend to have policy objectives in mind based on previous election campaigns and goals. Goals usually formulated without the aid of district accounting and budget records. Obviously, goals that would be based on what happened in the political environment of the previous board of education election, not on generational district budgets. Of course, the board members tend to live from election to election, just like politicians in other places, while district administrators are essentially tenured officials, usually tenured teachers. There is little news here, except that this budget politics background is seldom visible on the ballot, especially concerning things like district revenue taxes and school vouchers.

In light of the above, it should be no surprise that district budgets tend to take on a life of their own (above), just like in most other places in government (at least). But school districts are *so* labor intensive that this effect is considerably compounded in its intensity, due to salary and fringe benefits costs, to such an extent that outsiders to the budget seldom realize.

These outsiders sometimes include board of education members themselves; and they usually include the voting public, even during heavily contested elections. In addition, the district budget builds a life of its own, over time, because it is composed of people funded on a generational time line on the basis of quantitative student enrollment as a level of effort subsidy from state modulated tax revenue and transfer payment income redistributions. From an insider budget standpoint, the district staff in the budget is spending the budget money primarily to fund their positions and benefits as opposed to any people expenses outside the budget; and, those (any) outsiders are mostly the board members and the students— which reside above and below the district budget respectively (there are minor board member and student funds in the budget, but this is a technicality).

And beyond this organic budget life (above) for public school districts, there are definite possibilities for an intra-year transferability of funds within the budget, as noted earlier. Once income or revenue funds and streams become established in the district budget, it is relatively easy to begin to move them around, either a little or maybe a lot. Recent work has shown that instructional incentive funds were rolled into general fund revenues in California so that district expenditures reverted to pre-incentive patterns with problematic effects, but the data for this research was available only for marginal budget changes over a relatively short period of time (Picus, 1991). This state wide evaluation complements the district case study example used (below) to show diseconomies of scale in the historical development of a school district budget but, the extent of its power is limited by the relatively small amount of the incentive funds involved at the margin of the ongoing district regular (program) fund (budget). This just further goes to show why (longitudinal) generational budget histories are so important in accounting for school district behavior with regard to the great majority of ongoing district funding as reflected in the budget. School vouchers can pass if the voting public can be brought to appreciate the discretionary nature of district funding given district operational whats and whys in a budget climate of economic cost-plus taxing and internal (district) budget preferences. The post-World War II developments in California merely make this easier to study and understand.

TAKING THE BUDGET APART: BUDGET DETAIL LISTINGS AND POSITION SUMMARIES

An absolutely essential part of the operational (whats and whys) understanding of a school district budget is a detailed knowledge of the personnel positions that are funded in (by) the budget. Again, the reason for this is common (sense) knowledge. Something like 80-plus percent (above) of a public school district budget can be found in salaries and fringe benefits. Every thinking community leader and concerned voter intuitively knows this. So, the basic budget questions for school districts are who is being paid by the district, how much do they cost, and where are they in the budget.

The answer is simple. All of these employees exist (on paper) by virtue of their listed positions in the detail budget so that their salaries can be paid out of budget line item appropriations. So, to figure out how and where budgeted (planned) personnel costs are being spent, one must have a detailed personnel position listing and a summary position listing by personnel job category that includes all district employees. Usually, this is done by job title and salary level within job title; and, this approach is the basis for the build-up method in the diseconomies study that follows. To do such a study, every position in a given area of the district budget must be available for scrutiny. Most important for study purposes is to find out where the position is in the district hierarchy (level) and what it is supposed to do (function and title). Not surprisingly, the following example study highlights the inherent bureaucratic predispositions of the public schools and the reliance on bureaucracies in public education (Chubb and Moe, 1990; Lieberman, 1993); but, this method is the only way that specifics can be proven beyond mere (but valid) generalities.

However, the above level of detailed budget information is usually well within the internal purview of individual school district budget administrators. Everyone knows that there is one district superintendent (and what the position costs the district) and that there are a certain number of teachers within a defined salary range (and maybe their total cost); but, it seldom happens that all of the district personnel positions are accounted for and displayed (detailed out) for the board and the public to examine during each annual budget review cycle. If this last event did transpire as an annual budget position approval injunctive process, it would probably be called zero-base budgeting; and, it is well known that this does not happen in the public schools (above).

Therefore, what the schools do, in the main, is to approve and establish annual budgets as additions and deletions to the previous fiscal year budget. This is also not a complete surprise, but the extent of it might be for most of the voting public. In the schools, this sort of incremental change accounting is called budget discipline and fiscal management. Almost all district personnel (detail) positions are buried in the previous year budget during any given budget cycle; thus, these positions are neither added or deleted. And, this becomes yet another reason why boards and voters need position detail listings by job title *and* position summaries by job category, so that they can follow changes in total personnel costs as well as changes in costs at the margin (Leftwich, 1979).

Now, the fixed costs and the marginal costs for personnel come from adding up the old position costs and the new position costs each year and comparing changes in the costs, numbers of position, and types (job categories and titles) of employees on the district payroll. On the other hand, the fixed (base) revenues and marginal revenues accruing to a district come (in the main) from adding up the old student enrollment and the new student enrollment, because public school districts are paid essentially, in one way or another, so much for each student per school year. When board members and voters hypothetically compared (above) personnel services costs as represented in positions to enrollment revenues as represented by students, they were evaluating organizational efficiencies; and, in the spirit of the Progressive Era (above), they were expected to practice a generalized preference for economies of scale in the delivery of educational services. Based on freshman economics and good government (above), they were going to look to serve increasing numbers of students at the same level of service with *relatively* smaller increases in the number of district employees, over time (Leftwich, 1979). How they were going to do this was simple. They were going to count all of the employees and all of the students in the school district every year.

If this counting were to occur at the district level, it would be part and parcel of the traditional, centralized district accountability of the Progressive Era (above). And, if it were detailed out school-by-school, it would be part of the now innovative reform called school-based management. Of course, neither level of accountability is mutually exclusive; but, so called restructuring of school districts and experiments in site-based management seldom emphasize counting the employees, comparing those generating direct and indirect costs, and relating these to total overhead costs to student enrollment (income). It is not possible to do any judicial counting at all if position detail listings and position summaries by school district office and site location are not provided to the board, and thus, to the voters for decision making purposes. Vouchers can pass if voters are provided with a listing of all school district employees, their job titles, school and site locations, duty statements, and salaries including fringe benefits.

HOW THE GROWTH OF THE PUBLIC SCHOOLS IN A CLIMATE OF ECONOMIC EXPANSION TENDED TO CREATE LATENT BUDGET RESERVES WITHIN ESTABLISHED DISTRICT PROGRAMS

Given the importance of personnel positions in the building and justification of public school district budgets and costs, the current basis of these budgets and costs should be reviewed in terms of historical trends for public school district budget building. This basis would be the level at which vouchers would cost into the system to seek voucher pricing levels and (perhaps geographical) price points. The growth in public education after World War II had (of course) a major impact on school district budgets; and, this impact can be viewed, in part, as a pervasive, passive driver in individual school district budget cycles and funding levels.

After World War II, it was relatively easy (easier) for the schools to get new funding; and, overall, this funding was from multiple sources (Lieberman, 1993). The schools also heavily worked this ease; and, this could have been called revenue articulation, but it was not seen as such at the time. It was labeled and seen as something like new dimensions in public education and the raising of educational standards across the board in the spirit (above) of comprehensive schools, enrichment programs and federal funds for public education (Guthrie, 1979; Monk, 1987; Chubb and Moe, 1990).[1]

Thus, boards of education, especially in medium and large sized districts, were encouraged to develop and fine tune their internal budget cycle mechanisms as a means to process ever increasing enrollments and income streams. As is well known, two (of many) marco or mega factors in this situation were the baby boom and post World War II prosperity, especially in places like California. In the Los Angeles (below) metropolitan area (and other places), these factors were additionally compounded by a tremendous geographical population growth. By 1950, the stage was set to massage big bucks, even as the Korean War exacerbated labor shortages in the schools.

As districts grew in an environment of increasing enrollments and relatively easy money, they developed an addictive appetite for adding personnel and services costs to their budgets throughout the annual budget cycle. In certain organizational divisions of a school district (below), amazing numbers of positions could be added over the years. In the sense of the post war local good government, these increased costs and services could do only good; and, then certainly, they could not do any harm. In fact, during this period, quality tended to be measured in terms of costs (inputs). Districts could rate themselves by faculty degree accomplishments, salary levels, student faculty ratios, facilities construction accomplishments, program levels and spectrums, per pupil expenditures, and so on. In economics and business organization studies, such factors are called input parameters or variables; but, in the public education milieu of the time they were accepted at face value as the way of the good (organizational) life which included the building of prudent institutional reserves (Cyert and March, 1963; Lawrence and Lorsch, 1967; Cohen, March and Olsen, 1972).

This environment of spending drivers acted to generate a developing substrata of budget surpluses (balanced annually) within school districts—especially those that were experiencing rapid and significant growth. These budget surpluses and institutional reserves (above) could be maintained within educational programs as staff services detailed out in the budget detail position listings and position summaries (above). So, when dealing with a current public school district budget, a major question in funds flows analysis should be the relative factors for these reserves and how they developed and were maintained over time. Unavoidably, the surplus reserves condition raises the related question of how these balances can be manipulated or transmuted during successive district budget cycles and how they can be related to present and past budget detail listings (above). Here, personnel appropriations have to be compared to those for district capital outlay, contracts, equipment, substitute teachers, and so on. At any rate, the nature of school district funding and labor intensity has dictated that the majority of developing reserves originate in the position detail listings of the budget (below). Further, understanding the building base of funds reserves requires a familiarity with certificated and non-certificated employee salary schedules and the accounting and administration of personnel positions budgeted on these schedules as they relate to the budget cycle and board of education reporting practices. In addition, the reserves situation can get much more dramatic if and when the phenomenon of (board approved) unfilled, but budgeted, positions in the detail budget is brought into funds flow analysis. Suffice it to say that latent and significant budget reserves within established district programs became extant after the extended post World War II period of economic expansion and growth in the institutions of public education. The special importance of this for the voucher issue of today is the general fact that this phenomenon has gone virtually unnoticed by the voting public over the years.

SCHOOL DISTRICT NUMBERS

While the detailed position listings in the budget may account for the vast majority of school district expenditures and whereas these expenditures are going to involve a certain degree of latent reserves generation depending upon the historical circumstances involved for any particular district, yearly school district manning requirements must remain at the very core of board of education determination and responsibility. Some manning requirements are absolutely essential, and some are discretionary to one degree or another. In the case of such things as school district curriculum management responsibilities (below), it would be a judgement of the board as to district needs and the degree of discretion involved. For vouchers, the most important item in the detail budget for voters to consider is the number of teachers. The second most important thing for the voters to consider is the personnel that are listed in the detail budget besides teachers—how many, what kind, and how much they cost.

If a public school district had 60,000 full-time students, it would be said to have 60K Average Daily Attendance (ADA). This is the ADA measure of school district size that is used in the following "diseconomies of scale" study example. In a hypothetical school district with 60K ADA and an average of (say) 30 students per class, the said district would absolutely have to have 2000 full-time teachers. That would mean that every one of the 2000 teachers would be in front of 30 students all day, every day, all school year. Everything else would be support, discretionary or otherwise. This is one of the reasons that the following, historical curriculum management diseconomies of scale study is so interesting, because this historical and internal district educational agenda can be isolated in its structure and effects (Lieberman, 1993).

The certificated (teacher) positions shown in the diseconomies study are examples of out-of-the-classroom instructional support, pure overhead. This is the absolutely gut level difference between quantitative numbers and qualitative numbers in public education—students to teachers as opposed to students and teachers (together) to all other support personnel.

Given the 2000 teachers in the hypothetical district above, it should be completely possible for a local board of education to figure out everything else it would need to run the district—bottom up. Even if there were a three percent administrative surcharge for administrative overhead, this hypothetical (purely certificated) district would have 2000 teachers, 60 administrators, one district superintendent, and a board of education. Every other certificated position would have to be justified separately on the basis of a special district need. And, a district could be just as special as it wanted to be if it had the funding to be such and a voter constituency to back it up. Of course, it has happened this way before, and this is not new (Toch, 1991).

Bottom-up budget building could be used for non-certificated positions as well. This is the district non-teaching support staff, often termed (in district-speak) classified and non-classified in the non-teacher (non-certificated) personnel system. These are the bus drivers, custodians, education aids, and so on. If there were 2000 teachers, there would be approximately 2000 classrooms; and, there could be maybe one custodian for every 10 classrooms. That would be approximately 200 custodians. And so it would go. Obviously, the total number of teachers and support personnel needed to serve a given number of students at a given level of effort is problematic; and, it is this service level that is usually the matter of contention and the policy area that is most subject to fad and fancy, as was the case for curriculum management and supervision (below) in the past in California. Vouchers can pass if school district voters are presented with the actual district employee numbers as compared to a reasonable bottom-up costing of district requirements based on student enrollment.

Public school district numbers taken from final budget position detail listings can be the most powerful new tool for the voucher issue and the school-choice movement. This was one reason that the diseconomies study chose to examine a subset of out-of-the classroom, above-the-classroom district positions that grew and prospered for at least a generation. Positions such as these (and more) are still there in almost all district budgets. In fact, there are usually a lot more positions (relatively) between the classroom teacher and the superintendent today than when the study example ended. Actually, the historical situation in California (Rowan, 1982) is absolutely fortuitous for vouchers—especially in urban and suburban California. Detail listings can be used to analyze any and all parts of school district budgets, just as in the diseconomies study that follows. And, it will be no surprise that the study reflects the organizational characteristics of a bureaucratic agency with a voluminous detail budget and an internal market economy (Chubb and Moe, 1990).

BUDGET FUNDING, EDUCATIONAL PRODUCTION, AND SCHOOL DISTRICT DISECONOMIES OF SCALE

As outlined above, the current funding basis and organizational rationale for the American public school system rests heavily on perceived economies of scale (above) in the administration of this system—especially in its large, urban concentrations. This economies of scale rationale is both historical and operational; and, it forms the basis for the political consensus that supports the ongoing mobilization of national resources to underwrite the schools and their avowed goals. The justification for the low horizon, or current expenditure budgeting, support of the schools is the microeconomic efficiencies brought to the schools by the theory of the firm (Leftwich, 1979) while investment and capital resource allocations find their justifications in the application of macroeconomics to education as a long term, capital factor of national production in its investment form (Ackley, 1978; Blaug, 1985; Solmon, 1985).[2] The drivers for the school district consolidation movement have also been based on organizational economies of scale (Cohn, 1972; Guthrie, 1979; Friedkin and Necochea, 1988) and the search for a production function in the schools has been based on derived efficiencies to education through the modulation of size effects inputs to enhance outputs (Kenny, 1982; Sengupta and Sfeir, 1986; Monk, 1989, 1992; Monk and Haller, 1993). Both the post World War II intensification of consolidation efforts in the schools and the persistent desire to discover production frontiers and functions relevant to educational outputs have been based on a deeper and concomitant belief that, overall, even larger units of educational production might result in further efficiencies and accrue additional educational benefits to the student population viewed as a national resource (Callahan, 1962; Tyack, 1974;

Fox, 1981). Taking this as a basis for departure, it would be valuable to examine the growth of a large and representative, urban school district economic and educational aggregate during a period of post World War II growth to determine how the economies of scale rationale was, in fact, applied to effect any inherent production possibilities for the large scale application of educational resources over an extended period of time. Size, resource, and organizational growth data within the curriculum administration function for the Los Angeles Unified School District (LAUSD) during the period 1946-1968 has been made available for this purpose; and, the following analysis exhibits diseconomies of scale for organizational inputs within the scope of this study, as based on this data.

Diseconomies for organizational resource factors bring into question more fundamental aspects of organization theory as they have been applied to mass education and other forms of large scale, institutional organizations, especially since World War II. This study allows for the examination of resource inputs (funding), size (student population), and organizational structure (hierarchy) for a significantly large aggregate of the factors of production in public education to enable a relevant comparison of the generic organization theory approaches to the relationship between size, structure, and function within organizations with the addition of possible funding frontiers (Kimberly, 1976). Most particularly, the study data calls into question the proposition of organizational size, measured by the average daily attendance (ADA) of the student population, as a causal antecedent of organizational divisions and levels, where structure retains some formal relationship to function (Blau, Heydebrand and Stauffer, 1966; Blau, 1970; Blau and Schoenherr, 1971; Meyer, 1972; Freeman and Hannan, 1975) but remains relatively undriven by funding factors. This last aspect is especially important to this study, because the data implies funding drivers exerting themselves upon an imperative hierarchy within a protected organization operating in the public sector (Bidwell and Kasarda, 1985, 1987). Thus, the study data directly address both the economies of scale rationale of the schools and the application of accepted principles of organization theory to these same schools where the economic and organizational factors of funding drivers seem to come into consequent play. Actually, it is the *extent* of the trends revealed in the study data that is most impressive.

STUDY DISTRICT DATA, METHODS, AND THEORY– AN EXAMPLE OF BUREAUCRATIC GROWTH IN THE PUBLIC SCHOOLS

Analysis of enrollment, budget, and organizational data for the LAUSD for the period 1946-1968 yields a picture of virtually monotonic increasing ADA, administrative hierarchy in central office curriculum management, and ADA derived budget. Yet, as ADA (and budget) grew (Figure 1), the hierarchy in curriculum grew (Figure 2) much faster than either, even given a full recognition of the high correlation between ADA and budget during the study period.

The reasons for this growth picture are several and manifold (above); but, for the purposes of this study, the fact that the central office curriculum hierarchy grew at a faster rate than the organizational size basis (ADA) and resource availability (budget) of the district is the substantive revelation. The comparison of Figures 1 and 2 illustrates the fact that the administrative rate of growth was being sustained by forces greater than probable client population demands or organizational resource potentials expressed in such parameters as bonding capacity, state funding and assessed valuation because the rate of such growth significantly exceeded that of both the growth in the presumable needs base and any comparable growth in derived organizational response requirements. Such a sequence of events is the opposite of that expected under a classical economies of scale analysis unless there were demonstrated increases in perceived educational outputs (test scores) during this organizational growth period; and, such output gains are known to have not been extant.[3] Thus, there is a case for organizational diseconomies of scale in resource application and utilization.

Comparing the above growth data with the known organizational and political environment for public education in California during the study period provides a more complete frame of reference with respect to organizational growth for the LAUSD. In so doing, both internal and external factors can be included in the study model without working out their detailed effects contribution in this finding. In the case of the LAUSD, the size and diversity of the District was such that it would be favorably reflective of state wide normative conditions, such as educational funding, institutional and political trends, and the ambient organization environment. This last factor might be termed the isomorphism potential available for the District to build upon (Meyer and Rowan, 1977; Meyer and Scott, 1983). Thus the District could be compared to the state population of public school districts in terms of political stability and environmental capacity for organizational growth. To further enhance the study objective, the growth in LAUSD central office curriculum management personnel depicted in Figure 2 can be dissected into its basic component categories by organizational level and function without analyzing, in this finding, specific support and task assignments within these categories. Figure 3 depicts the growth in administrative positions within four categories: senior administrator, supervisor, specialist, and consultant.

This data can be used to examine the organic growth aspects for the LAUSD organizational evolution during the study period; and, the questions relating to how and why these positions were created within the organization can be addressed. Thus, Figures 1, 2 and 3 graphically depict the District organizational growth in its size substrate, the impact this growth sustained in the management hierarchy for instructional curriculum as a line function in public education, and the organic development and composition of the expanding hierarchy, over time.

INSTITUTIONAL ENVIRONMENTS FOR PUBLIC SCHOOL DISTRICTS

The theory of institutional environments can be used as a basis to effect a normative background upon which to reflect the growth of the LAUSD curriculum management organization during the study period. A natural history perspective (above) can be used to analyze the isomorphisms between organizations and their institutional environments which abstracts administrative expansion as a growth process of organizational innovation that develops over time through the innovation of administrative services, their growth and diffusion during a period of institution building, and their stabilization and standardization within a given institutional environment (Rowan, 1982).[1]

Figure 4 depicts the chronicle of major events in the institutional environment for curriculum management in the state of California from 1935 to 1970 as those events were reflected in the percentage of California public school districts reporting central office curriculum management personnel (Rowan, 1982).[1]

Within this historical perspective, the period 1935-1950 can be seen as one of stabilized consensus and institution building where the institutional environment was in a condition of positive balance toward curriculum management innovation and diffusion with isomorphic effects being distributed throughout the State. Here can also be seen the growth of corporate schooling and organizational responsiveness to demands in the institutional environment for a curriculum pattern of control (above) in public education (Meyer and Rowan, 1978; Meyer, Scott and Deal, 1981).

Within the historical setting depicted in Figure 4, the Figure 3 data for the LAUSD shows the district initially (1945-1950) participating in the curriculum development consensus at only the senior levels and with only a limited number of curriculum dedicated positions. The same situation was the case going back as far as 1927 and 1936—Rowan's initial curriculum events for the State.[1] Thus, District resource expenditures in curriculum management were exhibiting certain economics of scale under conditions of moderate ADA growth (Figure 1) and extensive institutional diffusion (Figure 4) before, during, and just after World War II. This was the period during which the District looked to the past for administrative norms. Here, 1945 marks the return to normalcy after the war and the initialization of LAUSD organizational development while 1950 marks the maximum extent of institutional curriculum services diffusion in the state; but, the District continued to effect relative economies of scale in the face of rising enrollment and political consensus (Figures 1, 2, and 4).

In contrast, the period 1950-1970 can be seen as one of destabilized consensus and institutional building where the organizational environment was in a state of mild imbalance toward institution building in curriculum management with political forces in a condition of contention (Figure 4). The stage for this period of organizational development in the District was presumably set by the norms established in the 1935-1945 and 1945-1950 periods; yet, the District began an unprecedented expansion in its curriculum management level of effort without a corresponding chronicle of effects and events in the institutional environment as its justification. In fact, the size of the central office curriculum management function grew much more rapidly than the client base, as measured in ADA, and the additional revenues generated by this increasing size base and available to the organization for expenditure at a constant (percentage) level of effort. In addition, each of the curriculum management positions added during the study period increased salary and benefits expenditures at rates significantly above those of classroom teachers; so, increases in central office staff in relationship to ADA and budgeted funds meant that organizational resources that could have been used to directly support teaching were being transferred to subsidize the central office administrative function, at higher and increasing rates of expenditure. It seems plausible that discretionary, incremental or slack resources in the form of funding drivers played a role in these transfers and subsidies (Pfeffer, 1981). But, the result was that the factors and forms for diseconomies accruing to curriculum management were exacerbated, given the condition that perceived outputs were not increasing and institutional support for curriculum management (state wide) was eroding.

IMPLICATIONS FOR PUBLIC EDUCATION

The internal composition of the curriculum management categories in Figure 3 reveal that hierarchical growth occurred within almost all intermediate levels and specialized programs; so that, the resource allocation pattern of the overall curriculum function was repeated at lower levels across programs seemingly on the basis of internal needs and supply (Cohn and Hu, 1973; Monk, 1984, 1987). This implies a system of internal markets. Thus, the pattern in the Figure 3 data suggests a mechanical system of bureaucracy building as opposed to an open (dynamic, feedback) and environmental (Figure 4) system because it is so patently "top-down" in its derivation. Given that the funding basis for the District with respect to the positions studied was ADA generated and undifferentiated (general-fund), this pattern mitigates the application of organizational explanations based on administrative intensity and environmental constraint, funding fragmentation and school district complexity, technical complexities in the educational production process, and organizational complexity as a reflection of environmental complexity (Lawrence and Lorsch, 1967; Freeman, 1979; Chambers 1981; Meyer, Scott and Strang, 1987; Chubb and Moe, 1988). It seems that the curriculum management organization grew top-down, as vectored by funding or resource drivers, with only a tangential relationship to district organizational environment or size. It can still be inferred that the large increases in the use of educational professionals and specialists increased significantly the capacity of the district to interface with the organizational environment and its contingencies (Hannan and Freeman, 1978); but, it seems that these capabilities were primarily funding or organizationally derived even as they were presumably performance validated while, at the same time, they also served to exacerbate diseconomies in the production of educational outputs, per se. So, a large urban public school district can, and did, grow top-down with increasing performance diseconomies.

Not only are the public schools subject to the economics of politically articulated and protected funding, but they are favorably disposed to extensive external and internal myth creation coupled with a pervasive uncertainty in the technology of production (Cohen, March and Olsen, 1972; Cohen and March, 1974; Weick, 1976). Curriculum management is one of the organizational components of the public schools where the play of these two factors (myths and technology) can express itself to an impressive extent; and, an aspect of this is illustrated in the data set (Figure 4) titles themselves: superintendent (three levels) director, assistant director, supervisor (three levels), specialist, and consultant. In addition, there were also area, level, and subject position designators. The dominating norm for the incumbents of the Figure 4 positions during the study period was that of a District teacher with a masters degree in education, with each teacher having a varying background of experience in an instructional area and tenure in the District, and with each instructional arena subject to its own milieu of problematic preferences and unclear technology. As the District grew, each area and arena competed in the growth process in an environment of relatively undifferentiated funding, top-down; so that, at the end of the study period, each major segment of the functional organization was represented in its own right. This put a political perspective on the organizational design of District curriculum management as a system of interest coalitions and consolidations building on a substrate of discretionary resources, over time (Cyert and March, 1963; Pfeffer, 1978; Strang, 1987). And, not unexpectedly, the myth of title became a part of the management of meaning in the curriculum organization through a process of paradigm and shared belief creation in which resources were being perceived as focused upon outputs creation. So, it can be inferred that, in this case, school district diseconomies were pursued in an orchestrated pattern for organizational growth to achieve developing norms.

Beyond top-down funding drivers and the micropolitics of concentration and control in organizational development, there are implication in the study concerning the relationships between organizational size and environmental dependency. In this case, a relatively large organization like the LAUSD seemed to be less dependent on the institutional environment for legitimacy and resources than the smaller public school district organizations that are representative of the Rowan sample. Within institutional isomorphism, a large, powerful local organization could use its relational networks to mold the institutional environment to support its local structure. Large school districts, for example, often assign personnel (organizational lobbyists) to represent their organization at the state level. In California, their impact on the California State Education Code is reflected in numerous regulations aimed specifically at validating activities within large districts or relieving them from the burden that regulations governing more representative school districts might impose. This measure of influence makes change within the institutional environment less exogenous for large districts, such as the LAUSD, than that experienced by smaller, more organizationally dependent districts. There are also implications in the study concerning the relationship between organizational resources and organization organic development. In this case, a relatively large organization like the LAUSD seemed to exhibit funding driven organizational proclivities (beyond top-down) which could override incipient isomorphic and resource dependencies. So, it seems that income and wealth factors, beyond size (ADA) alone, can influence public school district abilities to accommodate, develop, and maintain organization structure given known isomorphisms within institutional norms.

DISECONOMIES CONCLUSIONS

The longitudinal nature of the LAUSD study data makes it possible to complement previous research using cross sectional data concerning school district attribute-building, hierarchy and vertical differentiation in relation to enrollment. In turn, this allows for a comparison of the differentiation of organizational production activities in the form of curriculum management with the economies for scale rationale in a setting of imperative hierarchy and protected revenues. The District growth model from a normalcy base and the absolute and relative District size made this comparison particularly substantive, especially when the Rowan model for institutional isomorphism with respect to curriculum management in the state of California is taken into account.

Within organizational boundaries dictated by the microeconomic theory of diminishing returns, economies of scale in the size of the central office curriculum management function would have been expected to be realized at some point in time as the District enrollment increased. This did not, in fact, occur during the study period; but, more importantly, the size and scope of the central office curriculum administration function continued to increase at an accelerating rate relative to the size of the student population and the amount of organizational revenue generated by the District over the same period. Thus, during the study period, the District was pursuing accelerating diseconomies of scale in the curriculum function even as the institutional environment was decelerating from its previous phase of institution building and political consensus, while the case for increases in perceived educational outputs remained moot. Vouchers can work to discourage diseconomies such as these.

The public school district map in Figure 5 illustrates the relative geographic and political situation for the public schools in Los Angeles County, California.

CURRICULUM EVENTS AND NOTES FOR DISECONOMIES

1. Chronicle of events in the institutional environment for the diffusion of curriculum management personnel in California (Rowan):

    1) 1927: California Curriculum Commission established by legislative act
    2) 1936: Curriculum Commission completes guidelines for curriculum
    3) 1938: Course of study adopted for mathematics
    4) 1939: State law provides for certification of supervisors of curriculum
    5) 1946: Mathematics curriculum revised
    6) 1946: Social studies curriculum adopted
    7) 1950: Social studies curriculum revised
    8) 1958: Federal law (NDEA) provides funds for science, mathematics, and foreign language instruction

2. Although important to secular trends in education viewed as a component of national production, capital and investment concerns can be taken as of minor consequence in the resource allocations covered in this study, primarily due to the current expense nature of school district funding. Even so, the capital stock in the school system is enormous and periodically changes through its net investment, which is taken to be gross investment minus depreciation. Yet, depreciation seldom figures prominently in the decision economics of education or the organization of the schools.

3. Under conditions of economies of scale returns, the growth of curriculum supervision would have been expected to initially increase more rapidly (perhaps) than growth in the size of the student population; but, after some point, it would have begun to slow its

rate of growth in relationship to that same growth in student population. The result would be an economies of scale with respect to the number of central office curriculum positions responsible for a given unit of ADA of pupil instruction. These economies of scale effects could have been maintained in all cases except that of a decline in output scores greater than a given marginal decline in the number of managers dedicated to curriculum.

BIBLIOGRAPHY

Ackley, G. (1978) *Macroeconomics: Theory and Policy.* New York: Macmillan Publishing Company.

Bidwell, C.E. and Kasarda, J.D. (1985) *The Organization and Its Ecosystem: A Theory of Structuring in Organizations.* Greenwich: JAI Press.

Bidwell, C.E. and Kasarda, J.D. (1987) *Structuring in Organizations: Ecosystem Theory Evaluated.* Greenwich: JAI Press.

Blau, P.M. (1970) A formal theory of differentiation in organizations. *Am. Sociol. Rev. 35*, 201-218.

Blau, P.M.; Heydebrand, W.V. and Stauffer, R.L. (1966) The structure of small bureaucracies. *Am Sociol. Rev. 31*, 179-191.

Blau, P.M. and Schoenher, R. (1971) *The Structure of Organizations.* New York: Basic Books.

Blaug, M. (1985) Where are we now in the economics of education? *Econ. Educ. Rev. 4*, 17-28.

Callahan, R.E. (1962) *Education and the Cult of Efficiency.* Chicago: University of Chicago Press.

Chambers, J.G. (1981) An analysis of school size under a voucher system. *Educ. Eval. Policy Anal. 3*, 29-40.

Chubb, J.E. and Moe, T.M. (1988) Politics, markets, and the organization of schools. *Am. Pol. Sci. Rev. 82*, 1065-1087.

Chubb, J.E. and Moe, T.M. (1990) *Politics, markets, and America's schools.* Washington D. C.: The Brookings Institution.

Cohn, E. and Hu. T-W. (1973) Economies of scale, by program, in secondary schools, *J. Educ. Admin. 11* (October), 302-313.

Cohen, M.D. and March, J.G. (1974) *Leadership and Ambiguity.* New York: McGraw-Hill.

Cohen, M.D., March, J.G. and Olsen, J.P. (1972) A garbage can model of organizational choice. *Admin. Sci. Q. 17*, 1-25.

Cyert, R.M. and March, J.G. (1963) *A Behavioral Theory of the Firm.* Englewood Cliffs, NJ: Prentice-Hall.

Freeman, J. (1979) Going to the well: school district administrative intensity and environmental constraint. *Admin. Sci. Q. 24*, 119-133.

Freeman, J. and Hannan, M.T. (1975) Growth and decline processes in organizations. *Am. Sociol. Rev. 40*, 215-228.

Fox, W.F. (1981) Reviewing economies of size in education. *J. Educ. Finance 6*, 273-296.

Friedkin, N.E. and Necuchea, J. (1988) School system size and performance: a contingency perspective. *Educ. Eval. Policy Anal., 10*, 237-249.

Guthrie, J.W. (1979) Organizational scale and school success. *Econ. Educ. Rev. 1*, 17-27.

Hannan, M.R. and Freeman, J.H. (1978) Internal politics of growth and decline. *In Environments and Organizations* (Edited by Meyers, M.W. and Associates). San Francisco: Jossey-Bass.

Kenny, L.W. (1982) Economies of scale in schooling. *Econ. Educ. Rev. 2*, 1-24.

Kimberly, J.R. (1976) Organizational size and the structuralist perspective: a review critique, and proposal. *Admin. Sci. Q. 21*, 571-597.

Lawrence, P.R. and Lorsch, J.W. (1967) *Organization and Environment.* Homewood, IL: Richard D. Irwin.

Leftwich, R.H. (1979) *The Price System and Resource Allocation.* Hinsdale, Dryden Press.

Lieberman, M. (1993) *Public education—an autopsy.* Cambridge, MA: Harvard University Press.

Meyer, J.W. (1983) Institutionalization and the rationality of formal organizational structure. *In Organizational Environments: Rationality and Ritual* (Edited by Meyer, J.W. and Scott, W.R.). Beverly Hills, CA: Sage Publications.

Meyer, J.W. and Rowan, B. (1977) Institutionalized organizations: formal structure as myth and ceremony, *Am. J. Sociol. 83*, 340-363.

Meyer, J.W. and Rowan, B. (1978) The structure of educational organizations. *In Environments and Organizations* (Edited by Meyer, M.W. and Associates). San Francisco: Jossey-Bass.

Meyer, J.W., Scott, W.R. and Deal, T.E. (1981) Institutional and technical sources of organizational structure: explaining the structure of educational organizations. *In Organization and the Human Services* (Edited by Stein, H.D.). Philadelphia: Temple University Press.

Meyer, J.W., Scott, W.R. and Strang, D. (1987) Centralization, fragmentation, and school district complexity. *Admin. Sci. Q. 32*, 186-201.

Meyer, M.W. (1972) Size and the structure of organizations: a causal model, *Am. Sociol, Rev. 37*, 434-441.

Monk, D.H. (1984) The conception of size and the internal allocation of school district resources. *Educ. Admin. Q. 20*, 39-67.

Monk, D.H. (1987) Secondary school size and curriculum comprehensiveness. *Econ. Educ. Rev. 6*, 137-150.

Monk, D.H. (1987) School district enrollment and inequality in the supply of classes. *Econ. Educ. Rev. 6*, 365-377.

Monk, D.H. (1989) The education production function: its evolving role in policy analysis. *Educ. Eval. Policy Anal. 11*, 31-45.

Monk, D.H. (1992) Educational productivity research: an update and assessment of its role in education finance reform. *Educ. Eval. Policy Anal., 4*, 307-302.

Monk, D.H. and Haller, E.J. (1993) Predictors of high school academic course offerings: the role of school size. *American Educational Research Journal, 1*, 3-21.

Pfeffer, J. (1978) The micropolitics of organizations. *In Environments and Organizations* (Edited by Meyer, M.W. and Associates). San Francisco: Jossey-Bass.

Pfeffer, J. (1981) *Power In Organizations.* Marshfield, MA: Pitman Publishing Company.

Picus, L.O. (1991) Incentive funding programs and school district responses: California and Senate Bill 813. *Educ. Eval. Policy Anal., 3*, 289-308.

Rowan, B. (1982) Organizational structure and the institutional environment: the case of public schools. *Admin. Sci. Q. 27*, 259-279.

Sengupta, J.K. and Sfeir, R.E. (1986) Production frontier estimates of scale in public schools in California. *Econ. Educ. Rev. 5*, 297-307.

Solmon, L.C. (1985) Quality of education and economic growth. *Econ. Educ. Rev. 4*, 273-290.

Strang, D. (1987) The administrative transformation of American education: school district consolidation, 1938-1980. *Admin. Sci. Q. 32*, 352-366.

Toch, T. (1991) *In the name of excellence: the struggle to reform the nation's schools, why it's failing, and what should be done.* New York: Oxford University Press.

Tyack, D. (1974) *The One Best System.* Cambridge: Harvard University Press.

Weick, K.E. (1976) Educational organizations as loosely coupled systems. *Admin. Sci. Q. 21*, 1-19.

FIGURES

FIGURE 1

GROWTH IN LOS ANGELES UNIFIED SCHOOL DISTRICT
STUDENT POPULATION

800
700
600
500
400
300
200
100
0

AVERAGE DAILY ATTENDANCE (ADA) IN THOUSANDS

45 46 47 48 49 50 51 52 53 54 55 56 57 58 59 60 61 62 63 64 65 66 67 68

YEAR

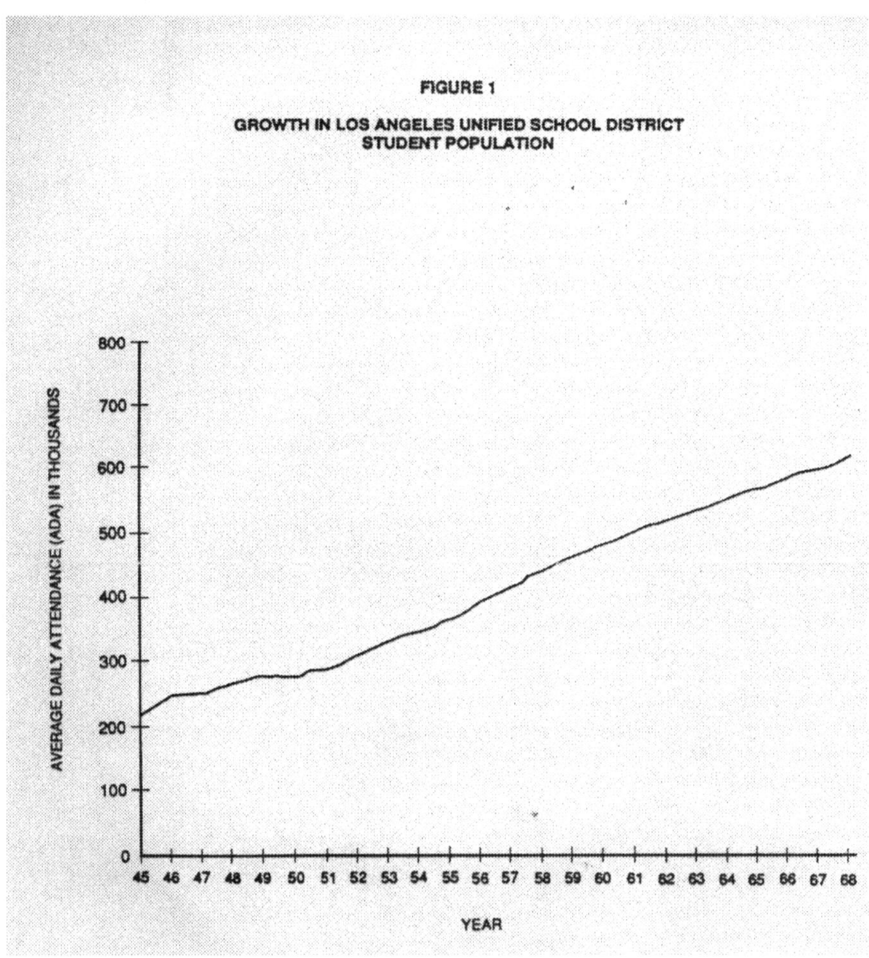

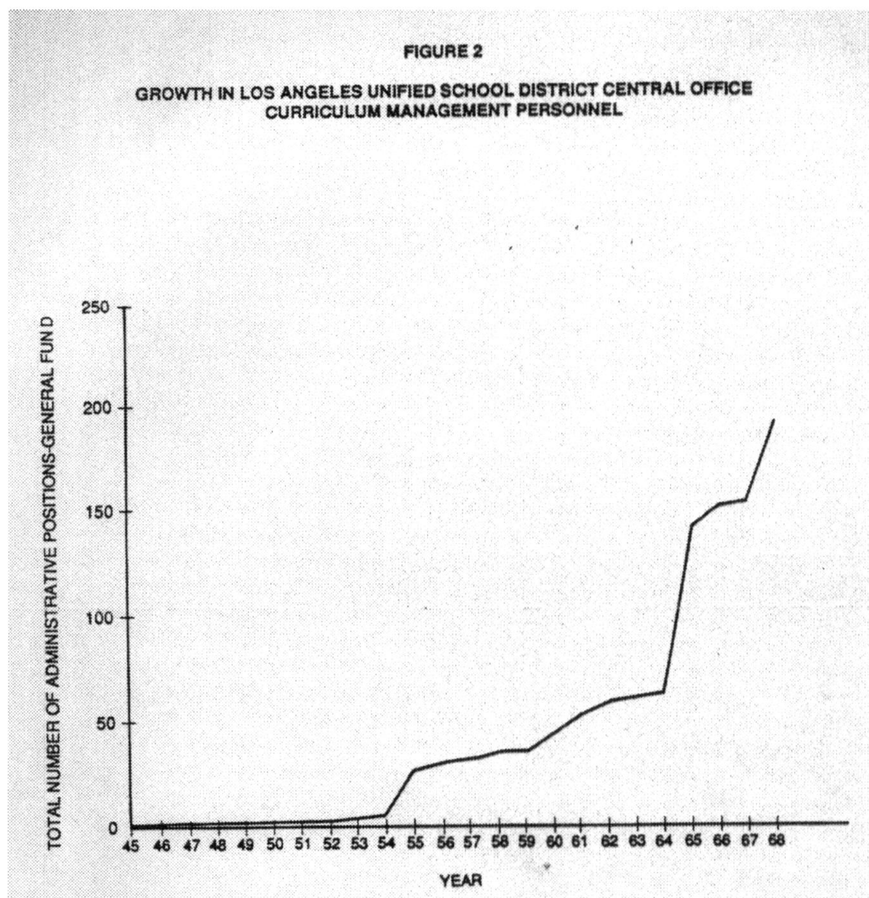
FIGURE 2
GROWTH IN LOS ANGELES UNIFIED SCHOOL DISTRICT CENTRAL OFFICE
CURRICULUM MANAGEMENT PERSONNEL
TOTAL NUMBER OF ADMINISTRATIVE POSITIONS-GENERAL FUND
250
200
150
100
50
0
45 46 47 48 49 50 51 52 53 54 55 56 57 58 59 60 61 62 63 64 65 66 67 68
YEAR

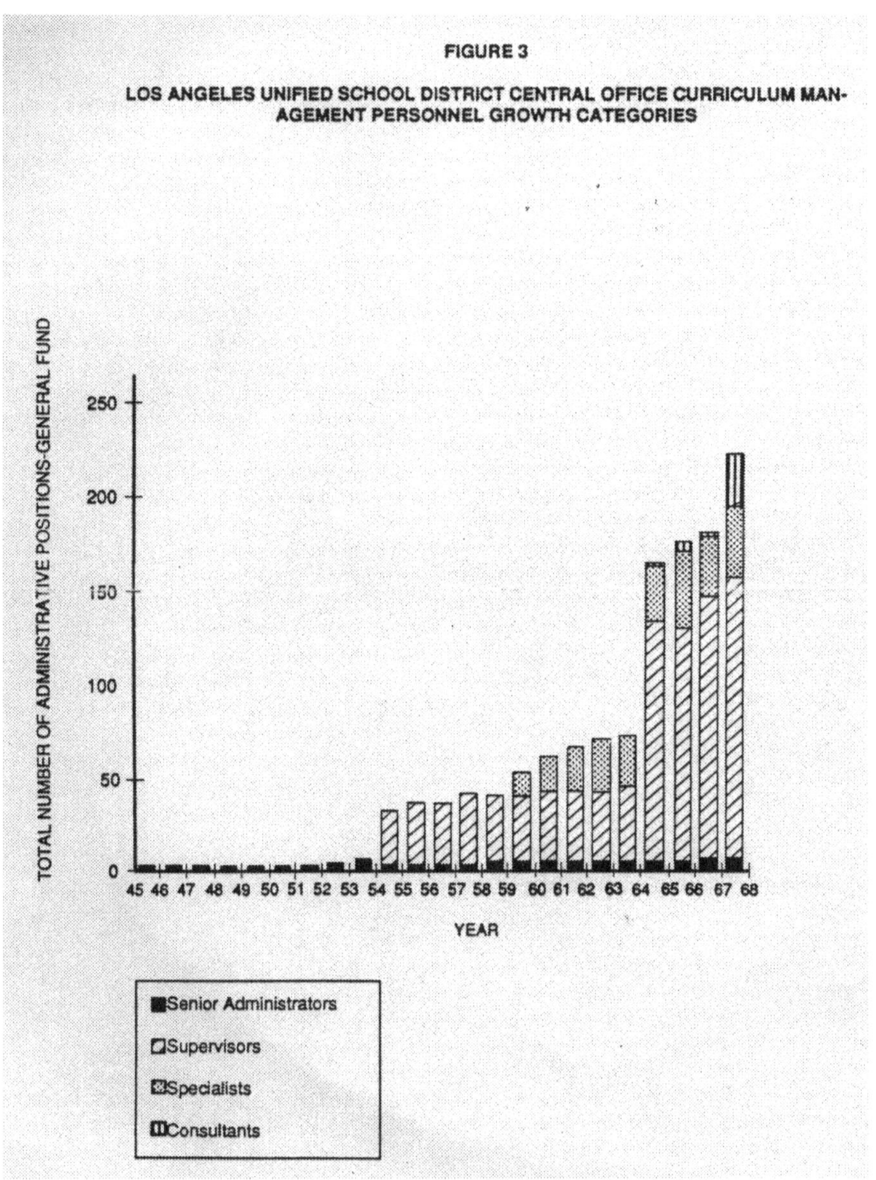
FIGURE 3
LOS ANGELES UNIFIED SCHOOL DISTRICT CENTRAL OFFICE CURRICULUM MAN-
AGEMENT PERSONNEL GROWTH CATEGORIES
TOTAL NUMBER OF ADMINISTRATIVE POSITIONS-GENERAL FUND
250
200
150
100
50
0
45 46 47 48 49 50 51 52 53 54 55 56 57 58 59 60 61 62 63 64 65 66 67 68
YEAR
Senior Administrators
Supervisors
Specialists
Consultants

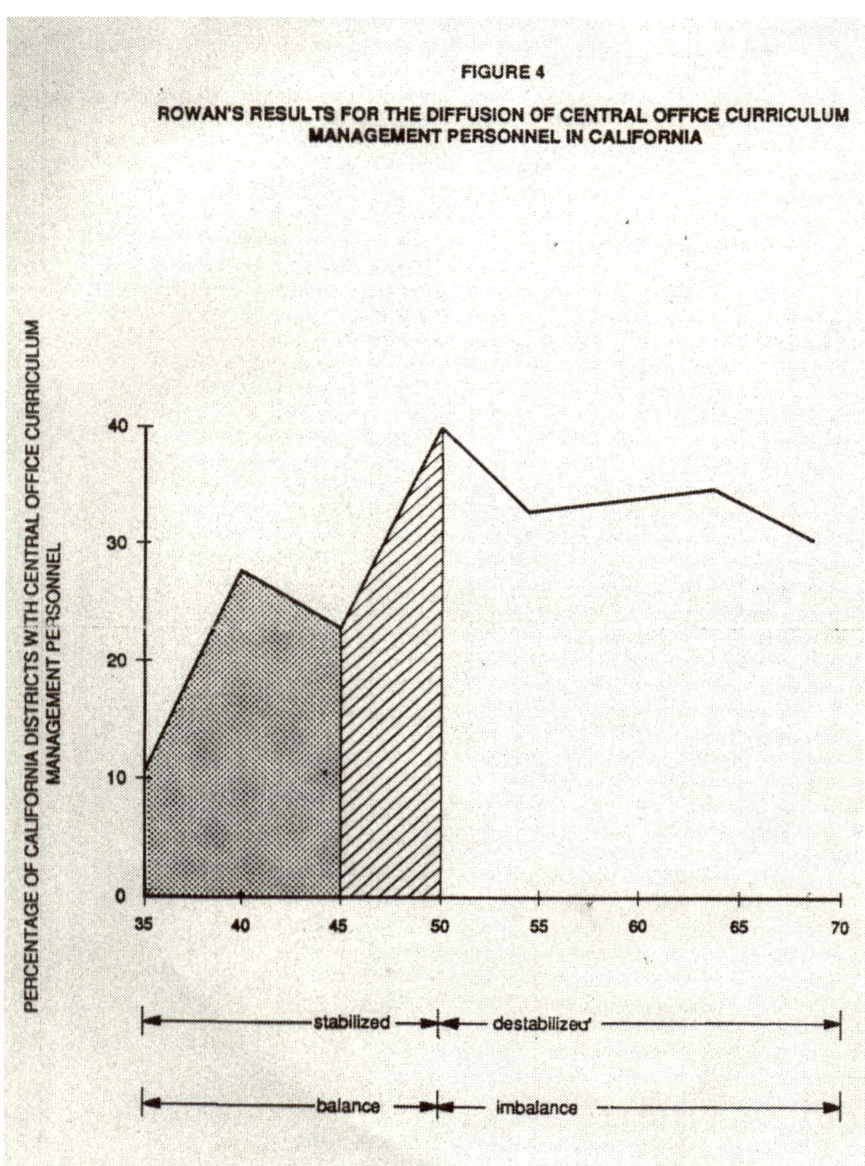
FIGURE 4
ROWAN'S RESULTS FOR THE DIFFUSION OF CENTRAL OFFICE CURRICULUM
MANAGEMENT PERSONNEL IN CALIFORNIA
PERCENTAGE OF CALIFORNIA DISTRICTS WITH CENTRAL OFFICE CURRICULUM MANAGEMENT PERSONNEL
40
30
20
10
0
35
40
45
50
55
60
65
70
stabilized
destabilized
balance
imbalance

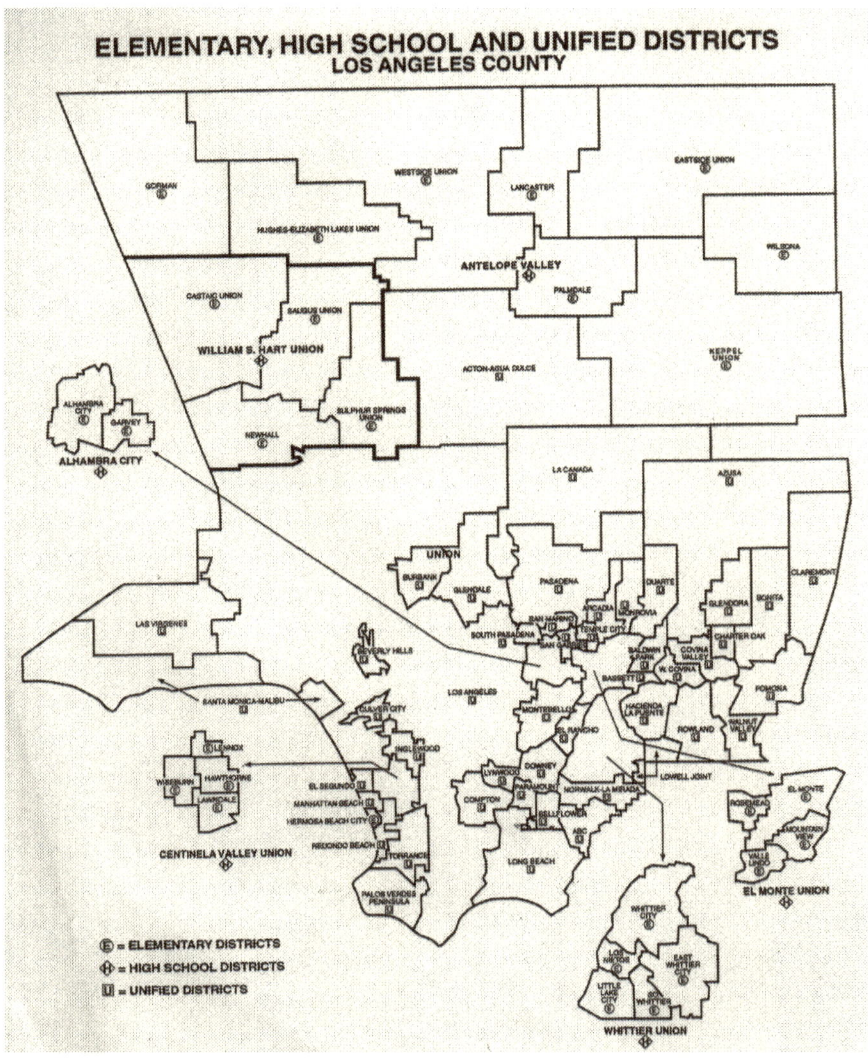

ELEMENTARY, HIGH SCHOOL AND UNIFIED DISTRICTS
LOS ANGELES COUNTY
GORMAN
WESTSIDE UNION
LANCASTER
EASTSIDE UNION
HUGHES-ELIZABETH LAKES UNION
WILSONA
ANTELOPE VALLEY
PALMDALE
CASTAIC UNION
SAUGUS UNION
KEPPEL UNION
WILLIAM S. HART UNION
ACTON-AGUA DULCE
ALHAMBRA CITY
GARVEY
SULPHUR SPRINGS UNION
NEWHALL
ALHAMBRA CITY
LA CANADA
AZUSA
UNION
CLAREMONT
BURBANK
LAS VIRGENES
GLENDALE
PASADENA
DUARTE
GLENDORA
BONITA
BEVERLY HILLS
ARCADIA
MONROVIA
CHARTER OAK
SOUTH PASADENA
TEMPLE CITY
SAN MARINO
COVINA VALLEY
SANTA MONICA-MALIBU
SAN GABRIEL
BALDWIN PARK
W. COVINA
CULVER CITY
LOS ANGELES
BASSETT
POMONA
LENNOX
INGLEWOOD
MONTEBELLO
HACIENDA LA PUENTE
WISEBURN
HAWTHORNE
EL RANCHO
ROWLAND
WALNUT
EL SEGUNDO
DOWNEY
LOWELL JOINT
LAWNDALE
LYNWOOD
EL MONTE
MANHATTAN BEACH
PARAMOUNT
NORWALK-LA MIRADA
ROSEMEAD
HERMOSA BEACH CITY
COMPTON
MOUNTAIN VIEW
REDONDO BEACH
BELLFLOWER
VALLE LINDO
CENTINELA VALLEY UNION
TORRANCE
ABC
EL MONTE UNION
LONG BEACH
PALOS VERDES PENINSULA
WHITTIER CITY
LOS NIETOS
EAST WHITTIER CITY
LITTLE LAKE CITY
SOUTH WHITTIER
E = ELEMENTARY DISTRICTS
= HIGH SCHOOL DISTRICTS
U = UNIFIED DISTRICTS
WHITTIER UNION